A FIRST PUFFIN
PICTURE BOOK OF
Bible Stories

Annabel Shilson-Thomas
Illustrated by Barry Smith

PUFFIN BOOKS

For Hannah

J55.091/£5.99.

PUFFIN BOOKS

Published by the Penguin Group
Penguin Books Ltd, 27 Wrights Lane, London W8 5TZ, England
Penguin Books USA Inc., 375 Hudson Street, New York, New York 10014, USA
Penguin Books Australia Ltd, Ringwood, Victoria, Australia
Penguin Books Canada Ltd, 10 Alcorn Avenue, Toronto, Ontario, Canada M4V 3B2
Penguin Books (NZ) Ltd, 182–190 Wairau Road, Auckland 10, New Zealand

Penguin Books Ltd, Registered Offices: Harmondsworth, Middlesex, England

First published by Viking 1993
Published in Picture Puffins 1994
5 7 9 10 8 6 4

Text copyright © Annabel Shilson-Thomas, 1993
Illustrations copyright © Barry Smith, 1993
All rights reserved

The moral right of the author and illustrator has been asserted

Filmset in Monotype Bembo Schoolbook

Made and printed in Italy by Printers srl – Trento

INTRODUCTION

 The Bible is not one book, but a large collection of much smaller books, written by many different people. It divides into two parts, the Old and New Testaments. The Old Testament covers a period of nearly two thousand years and tells of the early history of the Jewish people. It shows how their search for their own identity became deeply linked with their search for God. The New Testament covers a much shorter period, about seventy years in all, but most of it focuses on the three years of the ministry of Jesus Christ. It shows how the early Christians saw in him not only the fulfilment of Jewish hope, but the hope of all people, Jews and Gentiles.

It is hoped that children of any faith, whether they be Jew, Christian, Muslim, Hindu or of no faith at all, will find here stories that will fascinate and enchant them. The Bible is full of episodes whose themes are as pertinent now as they ever were. In this selection children will be introduced to Moses, the great leader, who guides his people from slavery to freedom. They will learn about Ruth and Naomi, whose friendship overrides the barriers of race and culture. They will encounter some of the great prophets, whose opposition to injustice often gets them into trouble. In the New Testament stories they will meet Jesus, champion of the underdog, who has time for the old and the young, the sick and the poor. All these stories tell us something of the nature of the God of the Jewish and Christian faiths. The order in which they are retold is intended to help children to see how the Jewish and Christian understanding of God developed.

Many Old Testament stories circulated by word of mouth for hundreds of years before being written down, and in some cases different versions of the same story were told. There is also a strong oral tradition behind the accounts of Jesus's life, death and resurrection found in the Gospels of Matthew, Mark, Luke and John. It was not until around forty years after Jesus's death that the first Gospel, Mark's, was written down. The retelling of Bible stories, then, is part of a natural process. It is hoped that the stories in this book will enable children to hear some of the best and most well-known Bible stories, perhaps for the first time, and go on to talk about them and retell them themselves.

Annabel Shilson-Thomas, 1992

In the beginning there were no likenesses of the women, men and events mentioned in the Bible. But since that time, of course, there have been many imaginative attempts by artists and writers to depict *their* version of events. The illustrations in this book attempt, in an accessible and my own personal way, to suggest the wealth of inspiration to be found in the Old and New Testaments.

Barry Smith, 1992

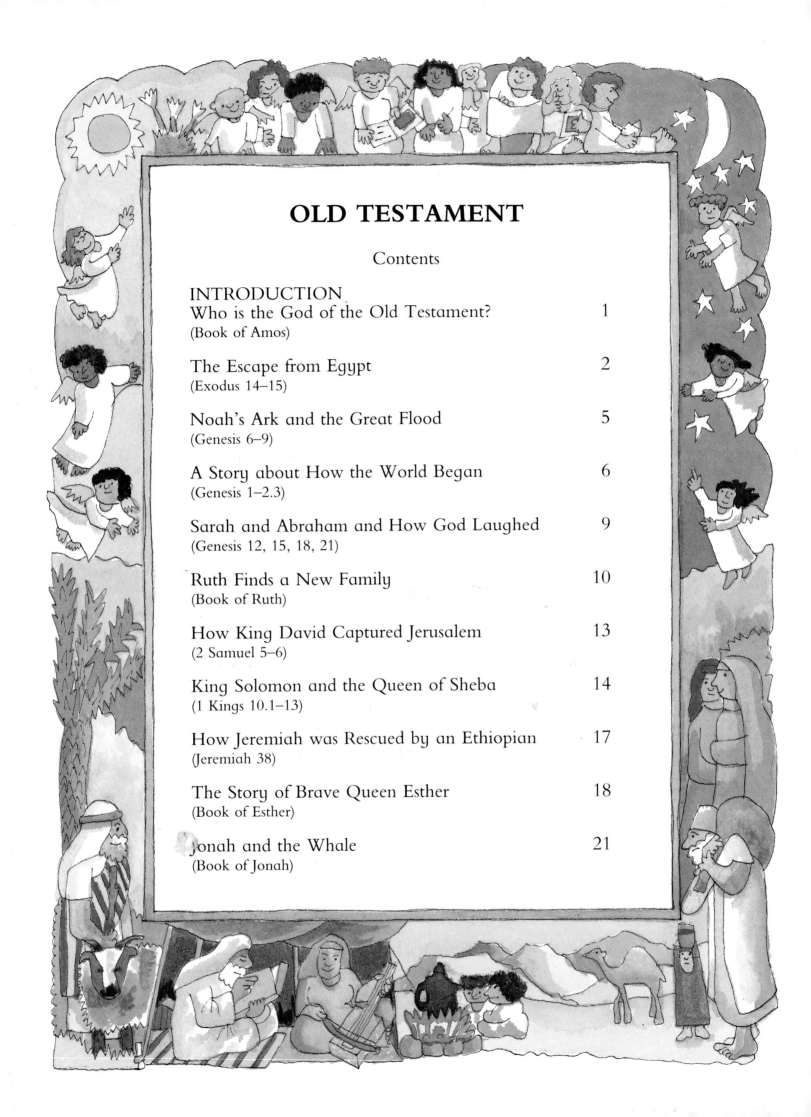

OLD TESTAMENT

Contents

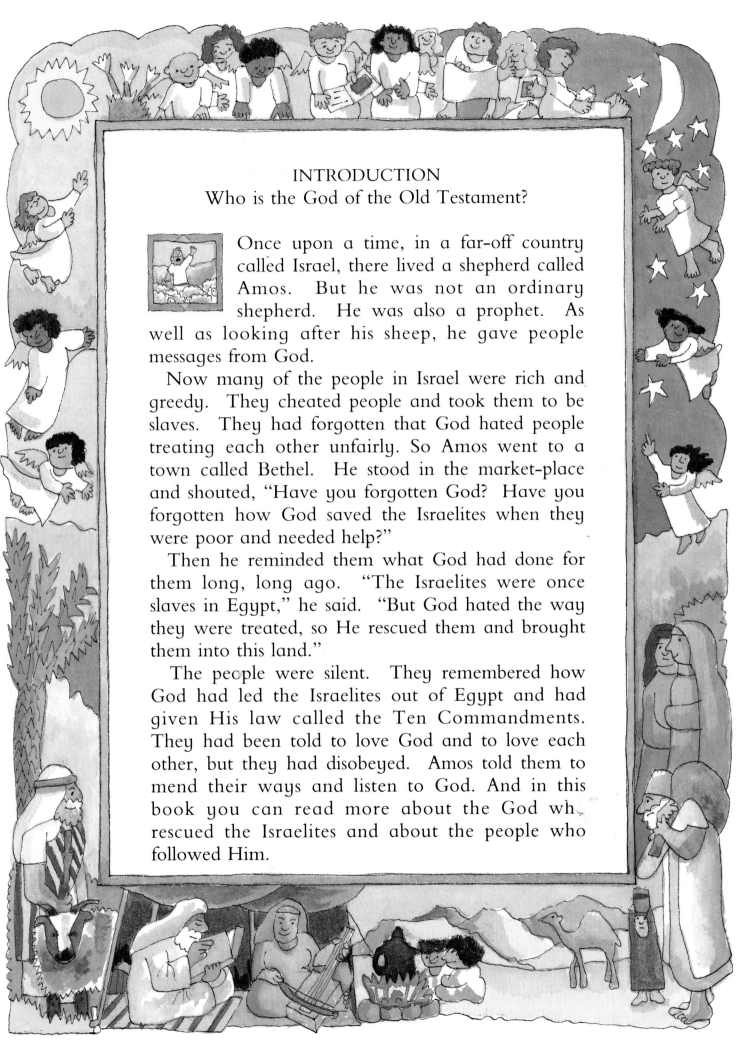

INTRODUCTION
Who is the God of the Old Testament?

Once upon a time, in a far-off country called Israel, there lived a shepherd called Amos. But he was not an ordinary shepherd. He was also a prophet. As well as looking after his sheep, he gave people messages from God.

Now many of the people in Israel were rich and greedy. They cheated people and took them to be slaves. They had forgotten that God hated people treating each other unfairly. So Amos went to a town called Bethel. He stood in the market-place and shouted, "Have you forgotten God? Have you forgotten how God saved the Israelites when they were poor and needed help?"

Then he reminded them what God had done for them long, long ago. "The Israelites were once slaves in Egypt," he said. "But God hated the way they were treated, so He rescued them and brought them into this land."

The people were silent. They remembered how God had led the Israelites out of Egypt and had given His law called the Ten Commandments. They had been told to love God and to love each other, but they had disobeyed. Amos told them to mend their ways and listen to God. And in this book you can read more about the God wh. rescued the Israelites and about the people who followed Him.

1

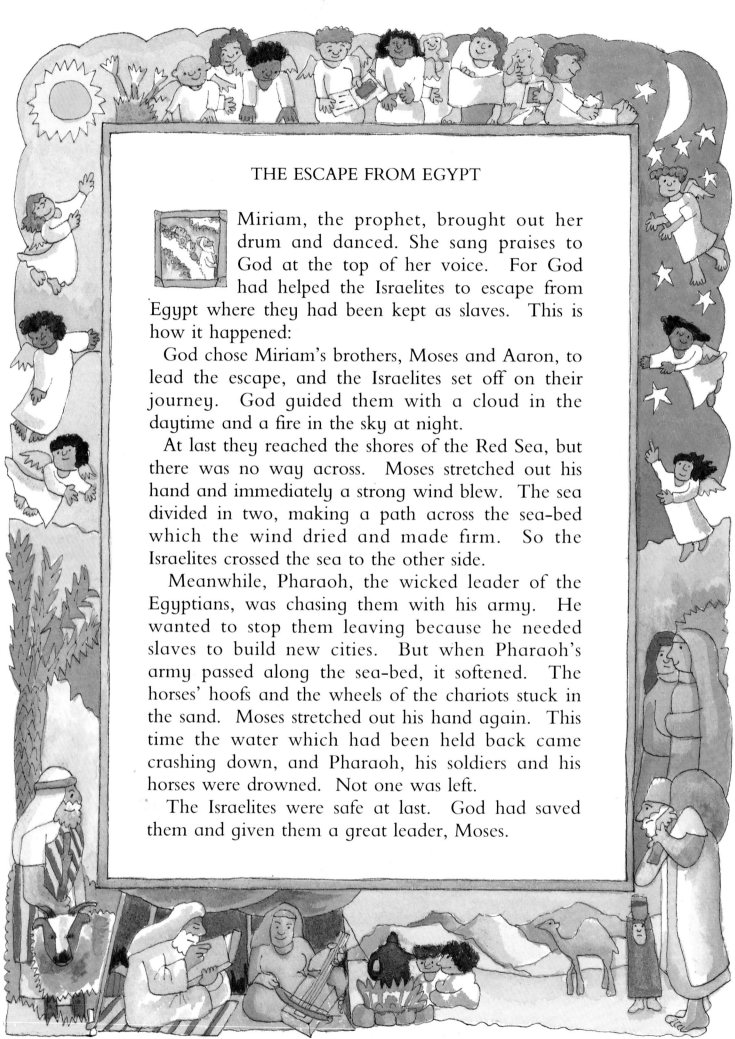

THE ESCAPE FROM EGYPT

Miriam, the prophet, brought out her drum and danced. She sang praises to God at the top of her voice. For God had helped the Israelites to escape from Egypt where they had been kept as slaves. This is how it happened:

God chose Miriam's brothers, Moses and Aaron, to lead the escape, and the Israelites set off on their journey. God guided them with a cloud in the daytime and a fire in the sky at night.

At last they reached the shores of the Red Sea, but there was no way across. Moses stretched out his hand and immediately a strong wind blew. The sea divided in two, making a path across the sea-bed which the wind dried and made firm. So the Israelites crossed the sea to the other side.

Meanwhile, Pharaoh, the wicked leader of the Egyptians, was chasing them with his army. He wanted to stop them leaving because he needed slaves to build new cities. But when Pharaoh's army passed along the sea-bed, it softened. The horses' hoofs and the wheels of the chariots stuck in the sand. Moses stretched out his hand again. This time the water which had been held back came crashing down, and Pharaoh, his soldiers and his horses were drowned. Not one was left.

The Israelites were safe at last. God had saved them and given them a great leader, Moses.

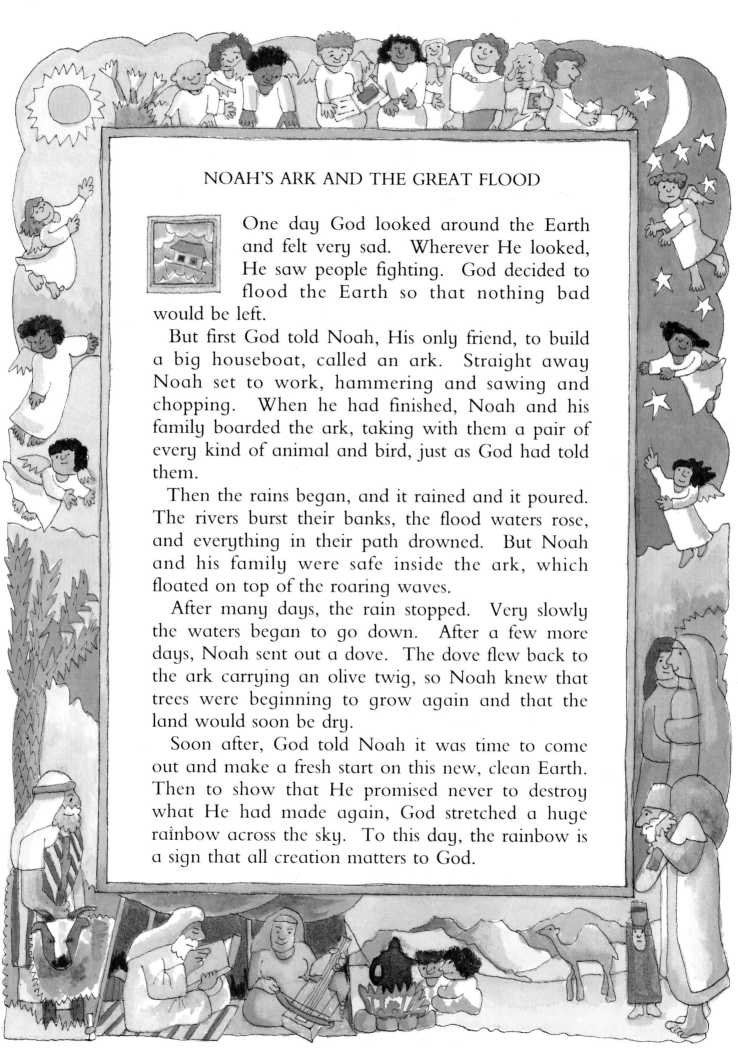

NOAH'S ARK AND THE GREAT FLOOD

One day God looked around the Earth and felt very sad. Wherever He looked, He saw people fighting. God decided to flood the Earth so that nothing bad would be left.

But first God told Noah, His only friend, to build a big houseboat, called an ark. Straight away Noah set to work, hammering and sawing and chopping. When he had finished, Noah and his family boarded the ark, taking with them a pair of every kind of animal and bird, just as God had told them.

Then the rains began, and it rained and it poured. The rivers burst their banks, the flood waters rose, and everything in their path drowned. But Noah and his family were safe inside the ark, which floated on top of the roaring waves.

After many days, the rain stopped. Very slowly the waters began to go down. After a few more days, Noah sent out a dove. The dove flew back to the ark carrying an olive twig, so Noah knew that trees were beginning to grow again and that the land would soon be dry.

Soon after, God told Noah it was time to come out and make a fresh start on this new, clean Earth. Then to show that He promised never to destroy what He had made again, God stretched a huge rainbow across the sky. To this day, the rainbow is a sign that all creation matters to God.

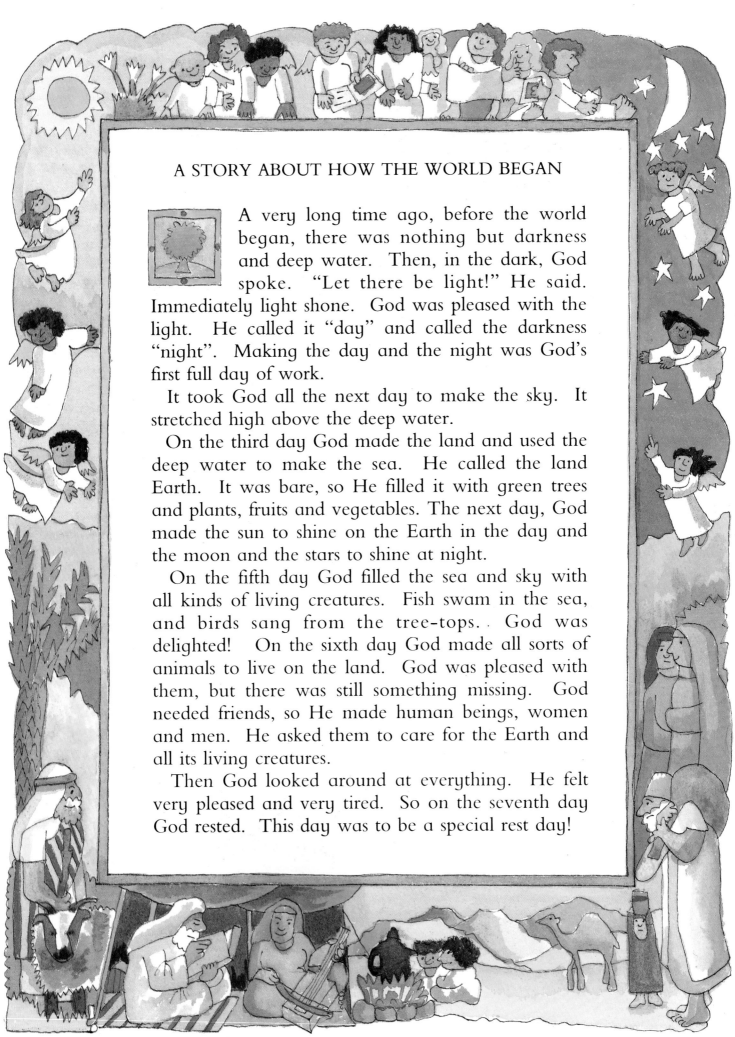

A STORY ABOUT HOW THE WORLD BEGAN

A very long time ago, before the world began, there was nothing but darkness and deep water. Then, in the dark, God spoke. "Let there be light!" He said. Immediately light shone. God was pleased with the light. He called it "day" and called the darkness "night". Making the day and the night was God's first full day of work.

It took God all the next day to make the sky. It stretched high above the deep water.

On the third day God made the land and used the deep water to make the sea. He called the land Earth. It was bare, so He filled it with green trees and plants, fruits and vegetables. The next day, God made the sun to shine on the Earth in the day and the moon and the stars to shine at night.

On the fifth day God filled the sea and sky with all kinds of living creatures. Fish swam in the sea, and birds sang from the tree-tops. God was delighted! On the sixth day God made all sorts of animals to live on the land. God was pleased with them, but there was still something missing. God needed friends, so He made human beings, women and men. He asked them to care for the Earth and all its living creatures.

Then God looked around at everything. He felt very pleased and very tired. So on the seventh day God rested. This day was to be a special rest day!

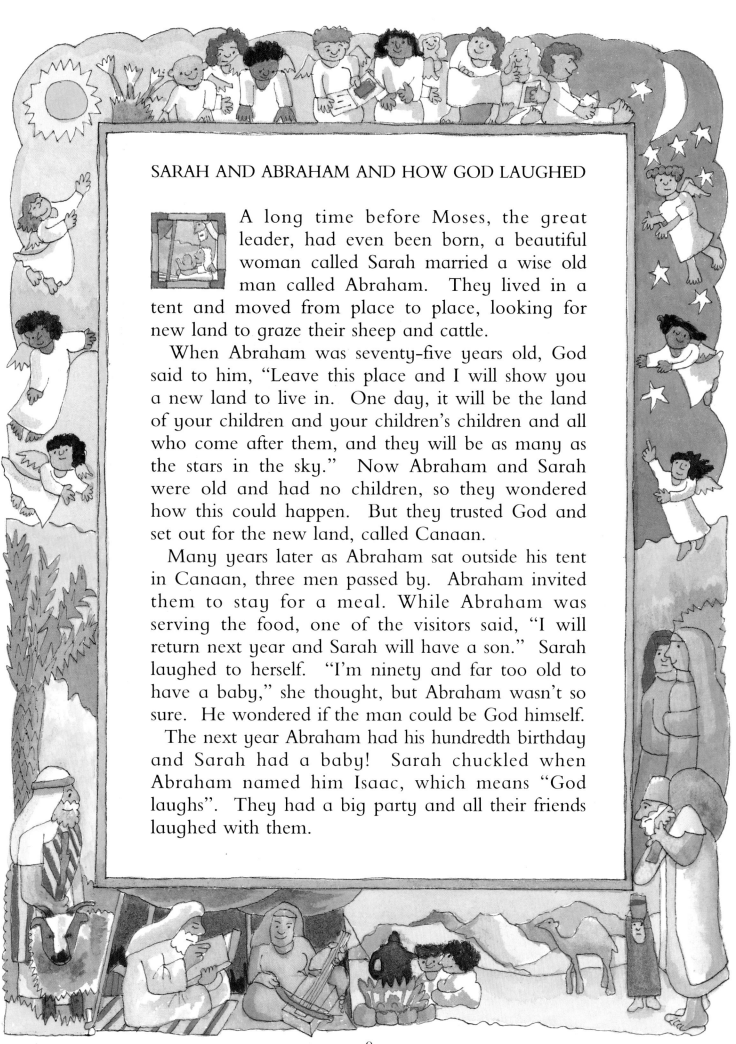

SARAH AND ABRAHAM AND HOW GOD LAUGHED

A long time before Moses, the great leader, had even been born, a beautiful woman called Sarah married a wise old man called Abraham. They lived in a tent and moved from place to place, looking for new land to graze their sheep and cattle.

When Abraham was seventy-five years old, God said to him, "Leave this place and I will show you a new land to live in. One day, it will be the land of your children and your children's children and all who come after them, and they will be as many as the stars in the sky." Now Abraham and Sarah were old and had no children, so they wondered how this could happen. But they trusted God and set out for the new land, called Canaan.

Many years later as Abraham sat outside his tent in Canaan, three men passed by. Abraham invited them to stay for a meal. While Abraham was serving the food, one of the visitors said, "I will return next year and Sarah will have a son." Sarah laughed to herself. "I'm ninety and far too old to have a baby," she thought, but Abraham wasn't so sure. He wondered if the man could be God himself.

The next year Abraham had his hundredth birthday and Sarah had a baby! Sarah chuckled when Abraham named him Isaac, which means "God laughs". They had a big party and all their friends laughed with them.

RUTH FINDS A NEW FAMILY

After the Israelites escaped with Moses from Egypt, they made their home in Canaan. This was the same land which God had shown Abraham and Sarah long ago. Now one year the crops did not grow in Canaan and there was not enough food for everyone. So a woman called Naomi and her family left Bethlehem, their village, and went to live in the land of Moab, far away.

Soon after they had arrived, Naomi's husband died. Naomi was sad and lonely. Then her two sons married two local girls called Orpah and Ruth and she cheered up because they became her friends.

Ten years later Naomi's sons also died. Naomi felt homesick and decided to return to Bethlehem, to the people of her own country. Now Ruth loved Naomi very much, so she left her family and went with Naomi. "From now on your people will be my people and your God will be my God," she told Naomi.

When they arrived in Bethlehem it was harvest time. A rich and kind man called Boaz noticed Ruth as she worked in the fields. The other workers told Boaz that she was a foreigner but Boaz did not mind that she was not an Israelite. He heard how she had cared for Naomi and he fell in love with her. Everyone rejoiced when Ruth married Boaz and had a son called Obed, and Naomi loved him as if he were her own child.

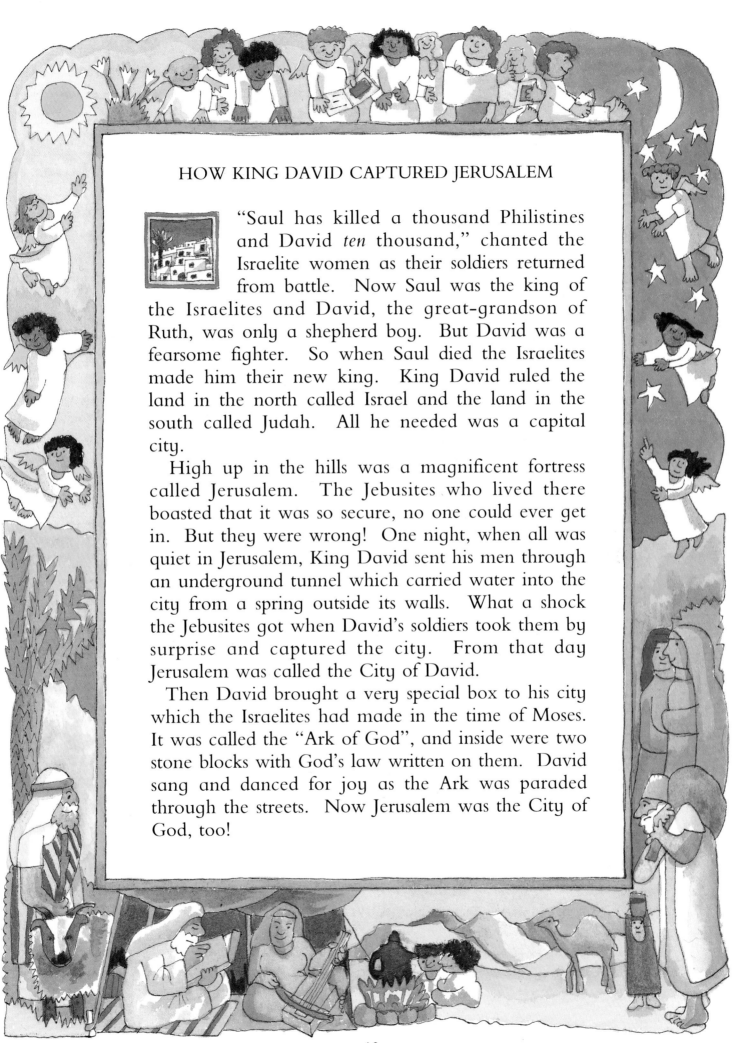

HOW KING DAVID CAPTURED JERUSALEM

"Saul has killed a thousand Philistines and David *ten* thousand," chanted the Israelite women as their soldiers returned from battle. Now Saul was the king of the Israelites and David, the great-grandson of Ruth, was only a shepherd boy. But David was a fearsome fighter. So when Saul died the Israelites made him their new king. King David ruled the land in the north called Israel and the land in the south called Judah. All he needed was a capital city.

High up in the hills was a magnificent fortress called Jerusalem. The Jebusites who lived there boasted that it was so secure, no one could ever get in. But they were wrong! One night, when all was quiet in Jerusalem, King David sent his men through an underground tunnel which carried water into the city from a spring outside its walls. What a shock the Jebusites got when David's soldiers took them by surprise and captured the city. From that day Jerusalem was called the City of David.

Then David brought a very special box to his city which the Israelites had made in the time of Moses. It was called the "Ark of God", and inside were two stone blocks with God's law written on them. David sang and danced for joy as the Ark was paraded through the streets. Now Jerusalem was the City of God, too!

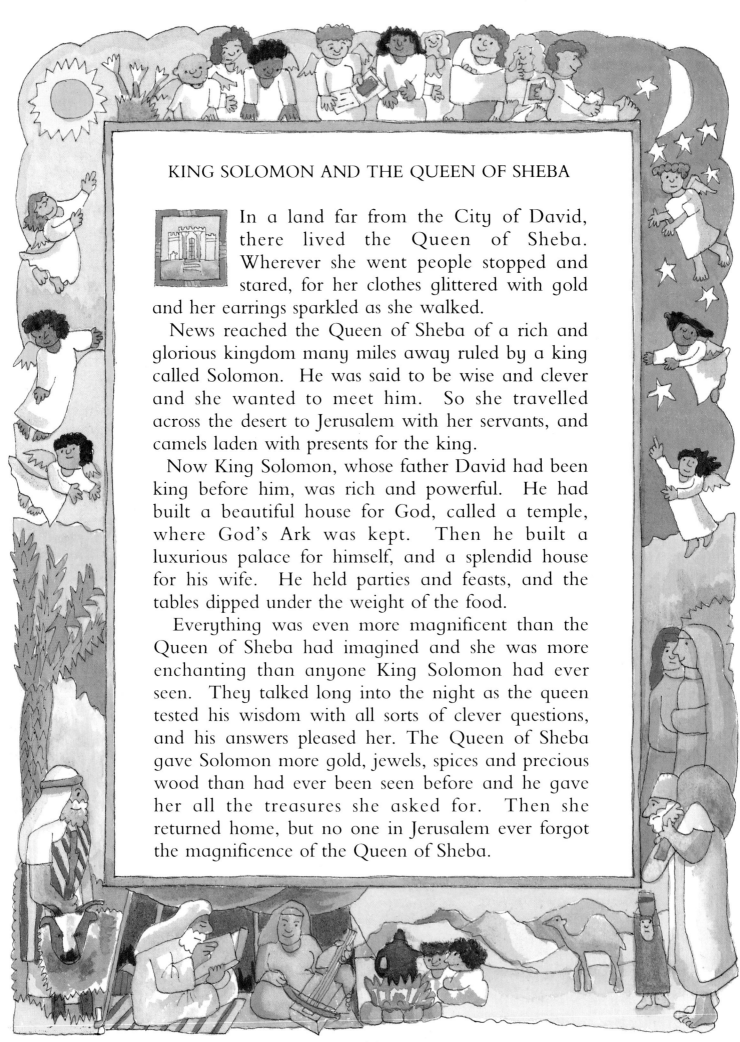

KING SOLOMON AND THE QUEEN OF SHEBA

In a land far from the City of David, there lived the Queen of Sheba. Wherever she went people stopped and stared, for her clothes glittered with gold and her earrings sparkled as she walked.

News reached the Queen of Sheba of a rich and glorious kingdom many miles away ruled by a king called Solomon. He was said to be wise and clever and she wanted to meet him. So she travelled across the desert to Jerusalem with her servants, and camels laden with presents for the king.

Now King Solomon, whose father David had been king before him, was rich and powerful. He had built a beautiful house for God, called a temple, where God's Ark was kept. Then he built a luxurious palace for himself, and a splendid house for his wife. He held parties and feasts, and the tables dipped under the weight of the food.

Everything was even more magnificent than the Queen of Sheba had imagined and she was more enchanting than anyone King Solomon had ever seen. They talked long into the night as the queen tested his wisdom with all sorts of clever questions, and his answers pleased her. The Queen of Sheba gave Solomon more gold, jewels, spices and precious wood than had ever been seen before and he gave her all the treasures she asked for. Then she returned home, but no one in Jerusalem ever forgot the magnificence of the Queen of Sheba.

15

16

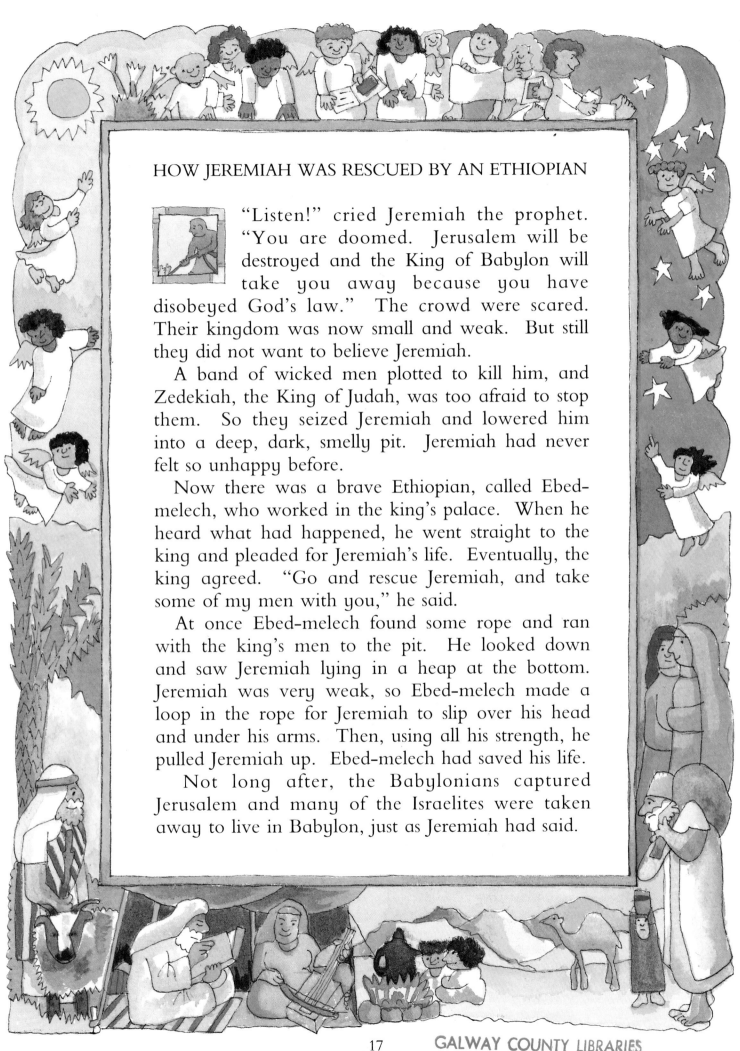

HOW JEREMIAH WAS RESCUED BY AN ETHIOPIAN

"Listen!" cried Jeremiah the prophet. "You are doomed. Jerusalem will be destroyed and the King of Babylon will take you away because you have disobeyed God's law." The crowd were scared. Their kingdom was now small and weak. But still they did not want to believe Jeremiah.

A band of wicked men plotted to kill him, and Zedekiah, the King of Judah, was too afraid to stop them. So they seized Jeremiah and lowered him into a deep, dark, smelly pit. Jeremiah had never felt so unhappy before.

Now there was a brave Ethiopian, called Ebed-melech, who worked in the king's palace. When he heard what had happened, he went straight to the king and pleaded for Jeremiah's life. Eventually, the king agreed. "Go and rescue Jeremiah, and take some of my men with you," he said.

At once Ebed-melech found some rope and ran with the king's men to the pit. He looked down and saw Jeremiah lying in a heap at the bottom. Jeremiah was very weak, so Ebed-melech made a loop in the rope for Jeremiah to slip over his head and under his arms. Then, using all his strength, he pulled Jeremiah up. Ebed-melech had saved his life.

Not long after, the Babylonians captured Jerusalem and many of the Israelites were taken away to live in Babylon, just as Jeremiah had said.

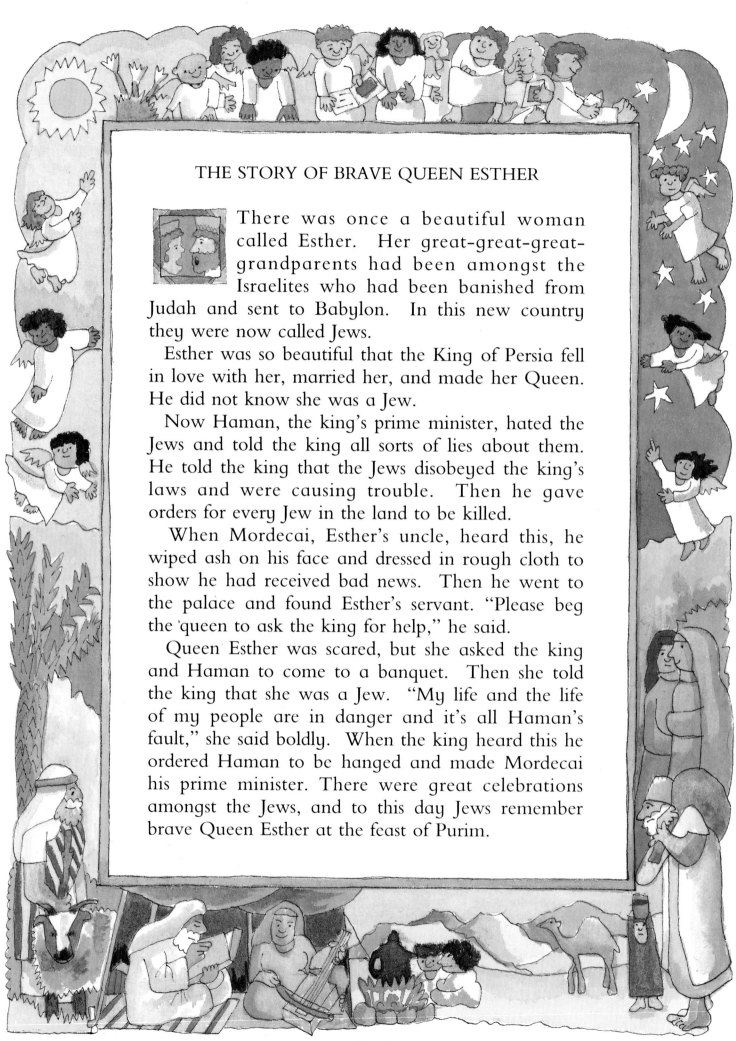

THE STORY OF BRAVE QUEEN ESTHER

There was once a beautiful woman called Esther. Her great-great-great-grandparents had been amongst the Israelites who had been banished from Judah and sent to Babylon. In this new country they were now called Jews.

Esther was so beautiful that the King of Persia fell in love with her, married her, and made her Queen. He did not know she was a Jew.

Now Haman, the king's prime minister, hated the Jews and told the king all sorts of lies about them. He told the king that the Jews disobeyed the king's laws and were causing trouble. Then he gave orders for every Jew in the land to be killed.

When Mordecai, Esther's uncle, heard this, he wiped ash on his face and dressed in rough cloth to show he had received bad news. Then he went to the palace and found Esther's servant. "Please beg the queen to ask the king for help," he said.

Queen Esther was scared, but she asked the king and Haman to come to a banquet. Then she told the king that she was a Jew. "My life and the life of my people are in danger and it's all Haman's fault," she said boldly. When the king heard this he ordered Haman to be hanged and made Mordecai his prime minister. There were great celebrations amongst the Jews, and to this day Jews remember brave Queen Esther at the feast of Purim.

19

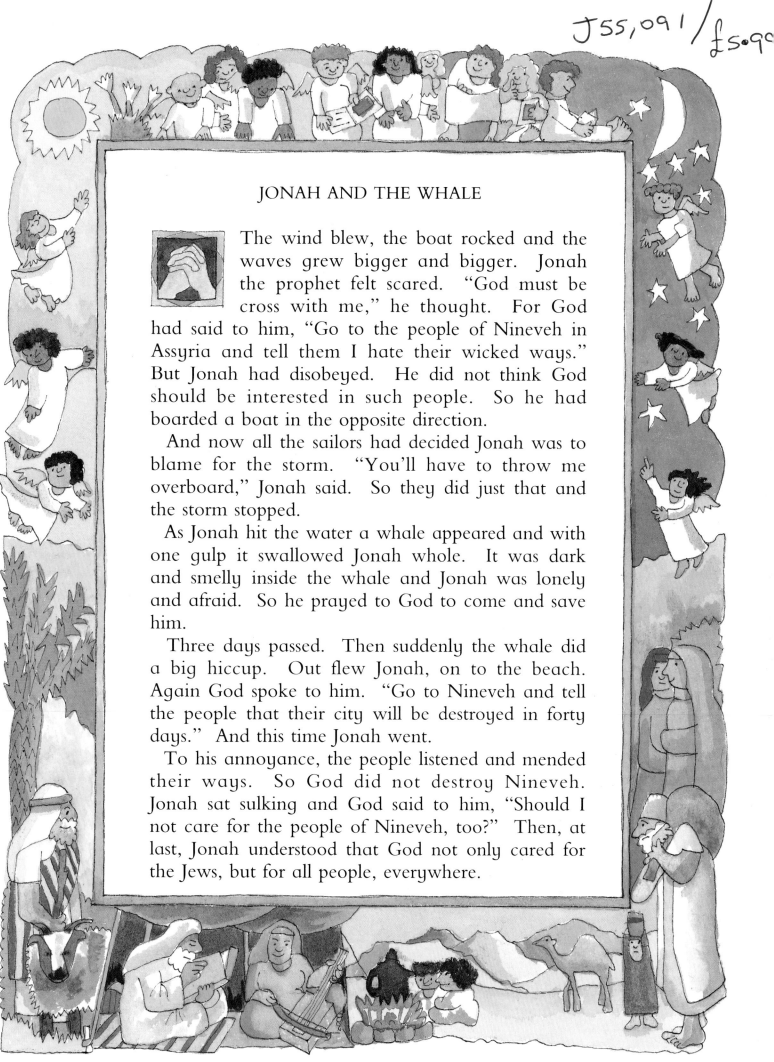

JONAH AND THE WHALE

The wind blew, the boat rocked and the waves grew bigger and bigger. Jonah the prophet felt scared. "God must be cross with me," he thought. For God had said to him, "Go to the people of Nineveh in Assyria and tell them I hate their wicked ways." But Jonah had disobeyed. He did not think God should be interested in such people. So he had boarded a boat in the opposite direction.

And now all the sailors had decided Jonah was to blame for the storm. "You'll have to throw me overboard," Jonah said. So they did just that and the storm stopped.

As Jonah hit the water a whale appeared and with one gulp it swallowed Jonah whole. It was dark and smelly inside the whale and Jonah was lonely and afraid. So he prayed to God to come and save him.

Three days passed. Then suddenly the whale did a big hiccup. Out flew Jonah, on to the beach. Again God spoke to him. "Go to Nineveh and tell the people that their city will be destroyed in forty days." And this time Jonah went.

To his annoyance, the people listened and mended their ways. So God did not destroy Nineveh. Jonah sat sulking and God said to him, "Should I not care for the people of Nineveh, too?" Then, at last, Jonah understood that God not only cared for the Jews, but for all people, everywhere.

NEW TESTAMENT

Contents

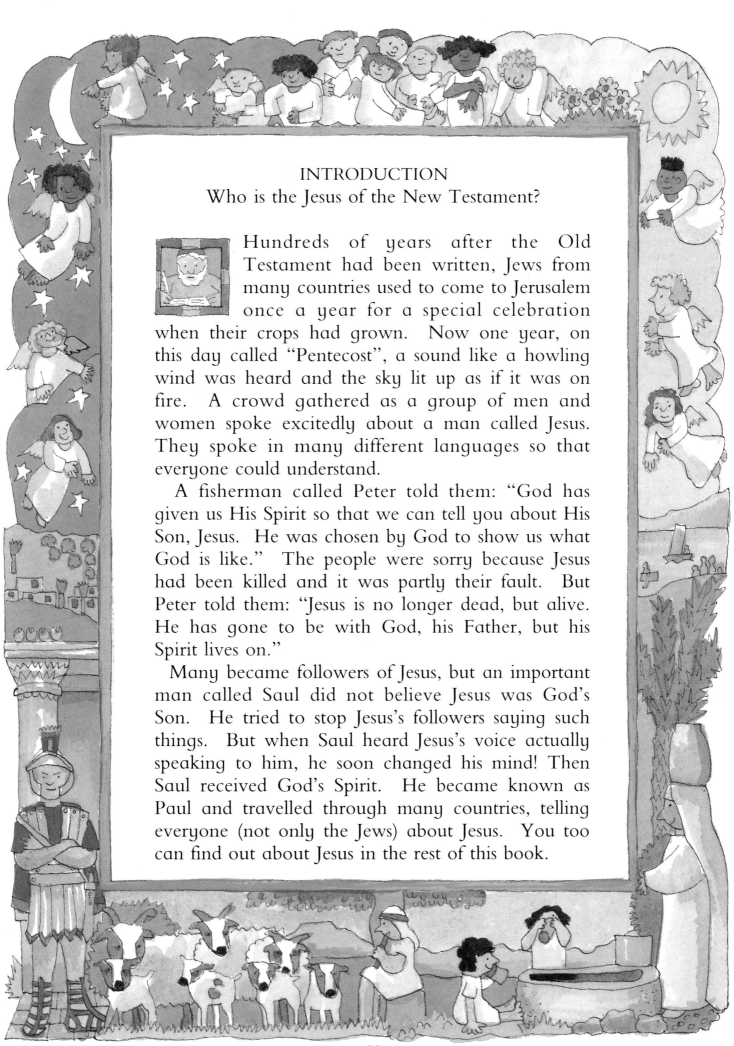

INTRODUCTION
Who is the Jesus of the New Testament?

Hundreds of years after the Old Testament had been written, Jews from many countries used to come to Jerusalem once a year for a special celebration when their crops had grown. Now one year, on this day called "Pentecost", a sound like a howling wind was heard and the sky lit up as if it was on fire. A crowd gathered as a group of men and women spoke excitedly about a man called Jesus. They spoke in many different languages so that everyone could understand.

A fisherman called Peter told them: "God has given us His Spirit so that we can tell you about His Son, Jesus. He was chosen by God to show us what God is like." The people were sorry because Jesus had been killed and it was partly their fault. But Peter told them: "Jesus is no longer dead, but alive. He has gone to be with God, his Father, but his Spirit lives on."

Many became followers of Jesus, but an important man called Saul did not believe Jesus was God's Son. He tried to stop Jesus's followers saying such things. But when Saul heard Jesus's voice actually speaking to him, he soon changed his mind! Then Saul received God's Spirit. He became known as Paul and travelled through many countries, telling everyone (not only the Jews) about Jesus. You too can find out about Jesus in the rest of this book.

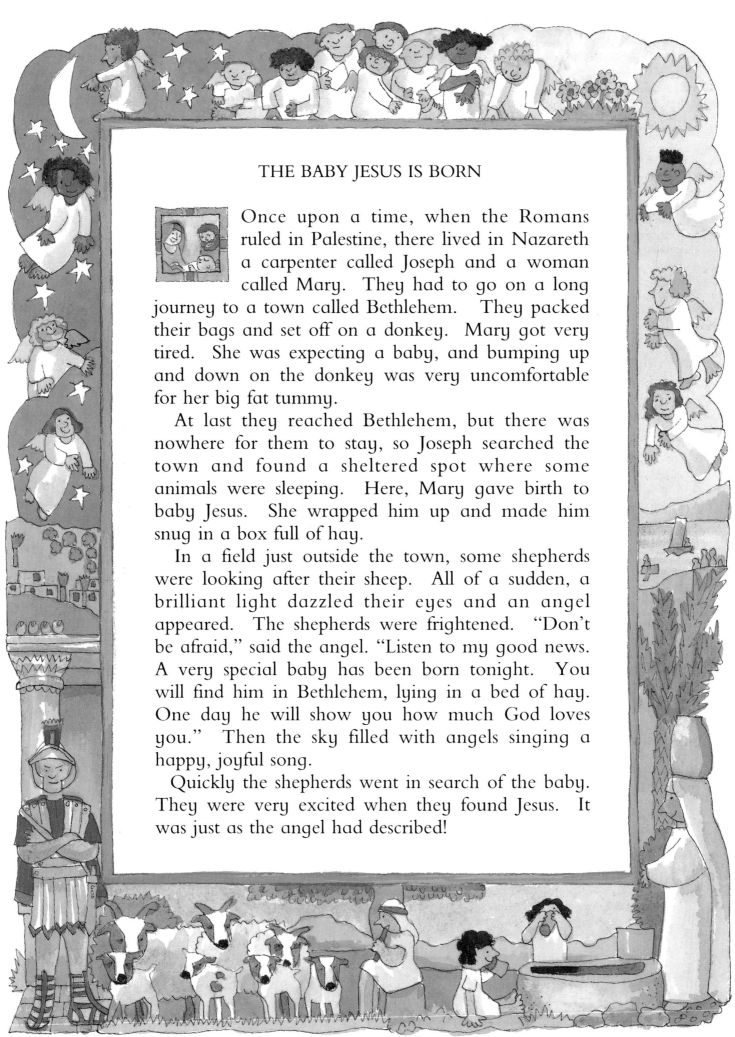

THE BABY JESUS IS BORN

Once upon a time, when the Romans ruled in Palestine, there lived in Nazareth a carpenter called Joseph and a woman called Mary. They had to go on a long journey to a town called Bethlehem. They packed their bags and set off on a donkey. Mary got very tired. She was expecting a baby, and bumping up and down on the donkey was very uncomfortable for her big fat tummy.

At last they reached Bethlehem, but there was nowhere for them to stay, so Joseph searched the town and found a sheltered spot where some animals were sleeping. Here, Mary gave birth to baby Jesus. She wrapped him up and made him snug in a box full of hay.

In a field just outside the town, some shepherds were looking after their sheep. All of a sudden, a brilliant light dazzled their eyes and an angel appeared. The shepherds were frightened. "Don't be afraid," said the angel. "Listen to my good news. A very special baby has been born tonight. You will find him in Bethlehem, lying in a bed of hay. One day he will show you how much God loves you." Then the sky filled with angels singing a happy, joyful song.

Quickly the shepherds went in search of the baby. They were very excited when they found Jesus. It was just as the angel had described!

25

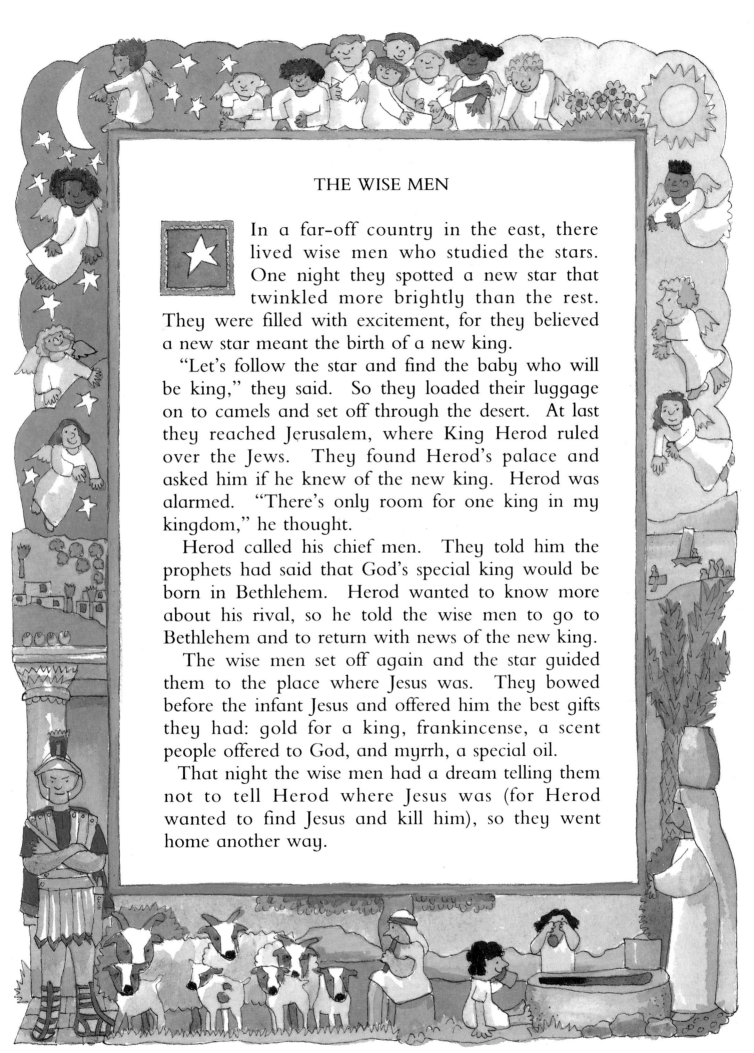

THE WISE MEN

In a far-off country in the east, there lived wise men who studied the stars. One night they spotted a new star that twinkled more brightly than the rest. They were filled with excitement, for they believed a new star meant the birth of a new king.

"Let's follow the star and find the baby who will be king," they said. So they loaded their luggage on to camels and set off through the desert. At last they reached Jerusalem, where King Herod ruled over the Jews. They found Herod's palace and asked him if he knew of the new king. Herod was alarmed. "There's only room for one king in my kingdom," he thought.

Herod called his chief men. They told him the prophets had said that God's special king would be born in Bethlehem. Herod wanted to know more about his rival, so he told the wise men to go to Bethlehem and to return with news of the new king.

The wise men set off again and the star guided them to the place where Jesus was. They bowed before the infant Jesus and offered him the best gifts they had: gold for a king, frankincense, a scent people offered to God, and myrrh, a special oil.

That night the wise men had a dream telling them not to tell Herod where Jesus was (for Herod wanted to find Jesus and kill him), so they went home another way.

JESUS IS BAPTIZED

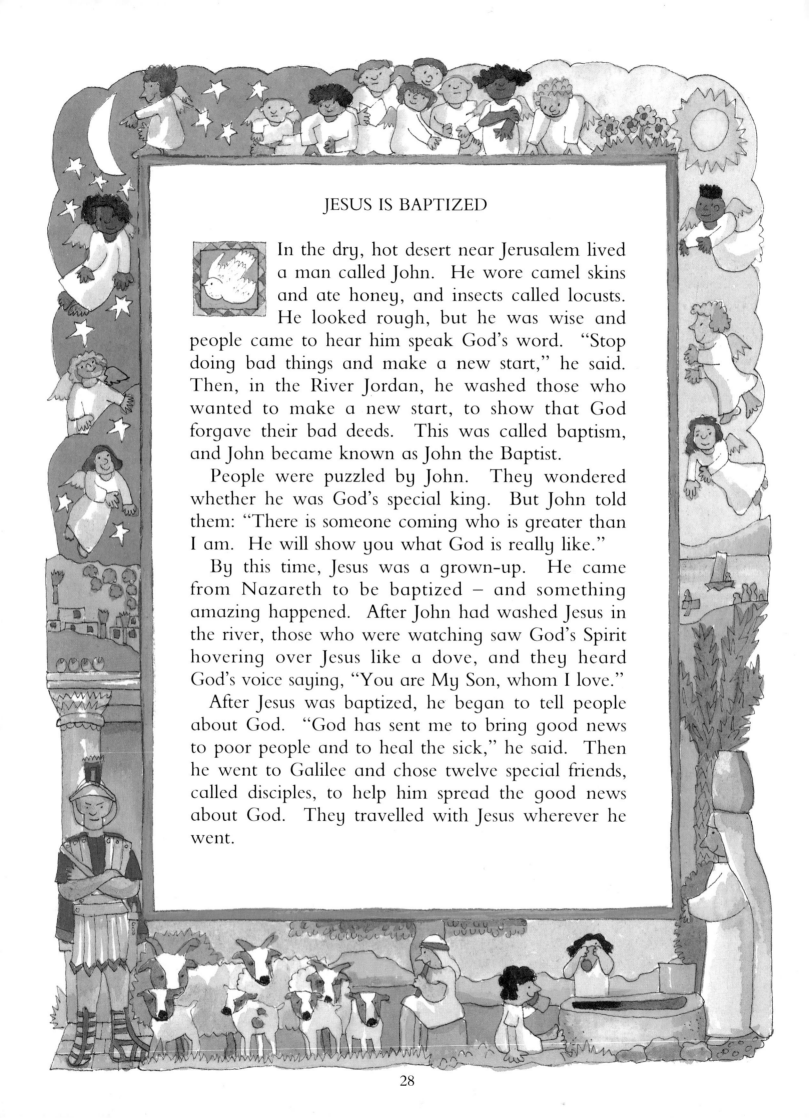

In the dry, hot desert near Jerusalem lived a man called John. He wore camel skins and ate honey, and insects called locusts. He looked rough, but he was wise and people came to hear him speak God's word. "Stop doing bad things and make a new start," he said. Then, in the River Jordan, he washed those who wanted to make a new start, to show that God forgave their bad deeds. This was called baptism, and John became known as John the Baptist.

People were puzzled by John. They wondered whether he was God's special king. But John told them: "There is someone coming who is greater than I am. He will show you what God is really like."

By this time, Jesus was a grown-up. He came from Nazareth to be baptized – and something amazing happened. After John had washed Jesus in the river, those who were watching saw God's Spirit hovering over Jesus like a dove, and they heard God's voice saying, "You are My Son, whom I love."

After Jesus was baptized, he began to tell people about God. "God has sent me to bring good news to poor people and to heal the sick," he said. Then he went to Galilee and chose twelve special friends, called disciples, to help him spread the good news about God. They travelled with Jesus wherever he went.

JESUS STOPS THE STORM

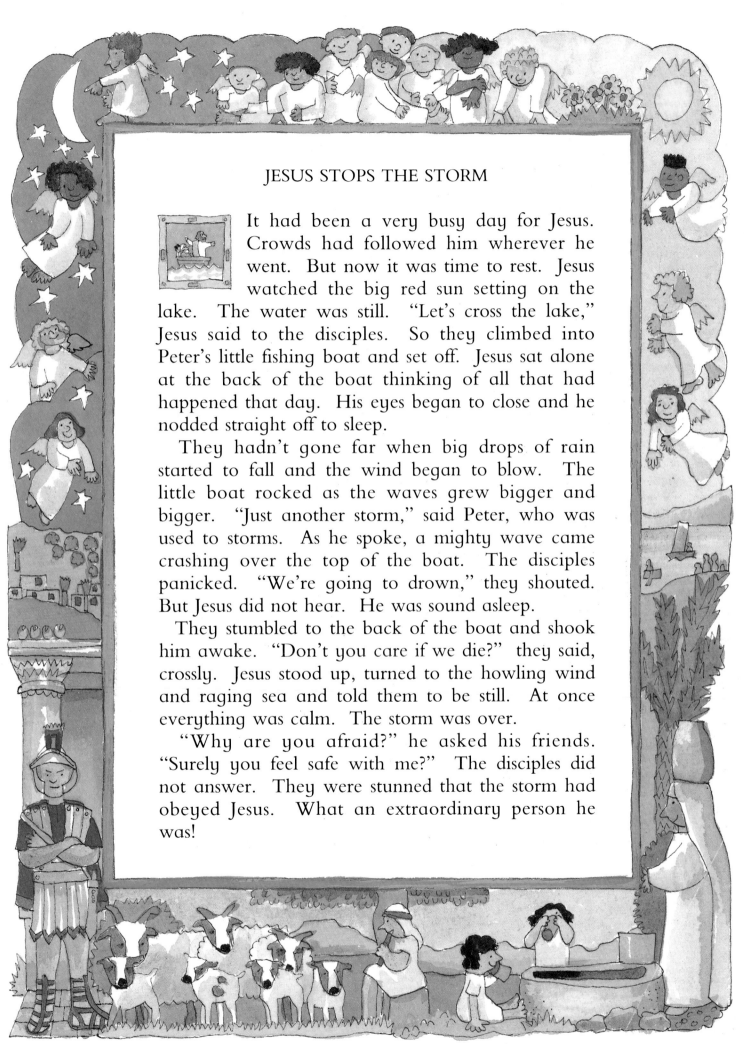

It had been a very busy day for Jesus. Crowds had followed him wherever he went. But now it was time to rest. Jesus watched the big red sun setting on the lake. The water was still. "Let's cross the lake," Jesus said to the disciples. So they climbed into Peter's little fishing boat and set off. Jesus sat alone at the back of the boat thinking of all that had happened that day. His eyes began to close and he nodded straight off to sleep.

They hadn't gone far when big drops of rain started to fall and the wind began to blow. The little boat rocked as the waves grew bigger and bigger. "Just another storm," said Peter, who was used to storms. As he spoke, a mighty wave came crashing over the top of the boat. The disciples panicked. "We're going to drown," they shouted. But Jesus did not hear. He was sound asleep.

They stumbled to the back of the boat and shook him awake. "Don't you care if we die?" they said, crossly. Jesus stood up, turned to the howling wind and raging sea and told them to be still. At once everything was calm. The storm was over.

"Why are you afraid?" he asked his friends. "Surely you feel safe with me?" The disciples did not answer. They were stunned that the storm had obeyed Jesus. What an extraordinary person he was!

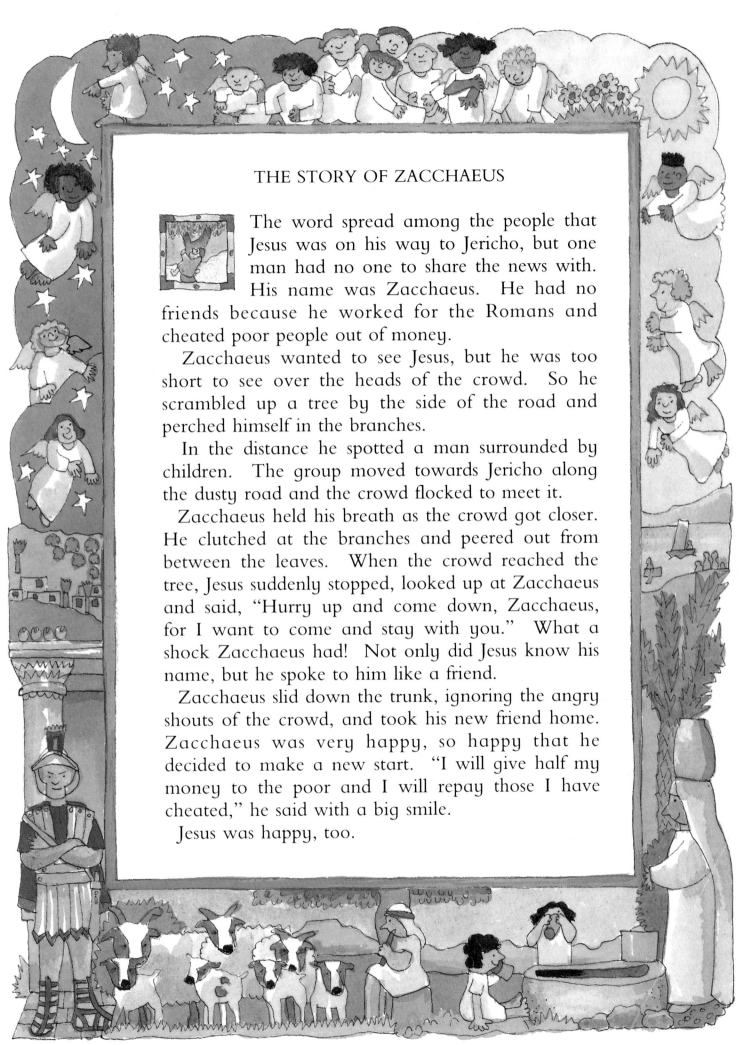

THE STORY OF ZACCHAEUS

The word spread among the people that Jesus was on his way to Jericho, but one man had no one to share the news with. His name was Zacchaeus. He had no friends because he worked for the Romans and cheated poor people out of money.

Zacchaeus wanted to see Jesus, but he was too short to see over the heads of the crowd. So he scrambled up a tree by the side of the road and perched himself in the branches.

In the distance he spotted a man surrounded by children. The group moved towards Jericho along the dusty road and the crowd flocked to meet it.

Zacchaeus held his breath as the crowd got closer. He clutched at the branches and peered out from between the leaves. When the crowd reached the tree, Jesus suddenly stopped, looked up at Zacchaeus and said, "Hurry up and come down, Zacchaeus, for I want to come and stay with you." What a shock Zacchaeus had! Not only did Jesus know his name, but he spoke to him like a friend.

Zacchaeus slid down the trunk, ignoring the angry shouts of the crowd, and took his new friend home. Zacchaeus was very happy, so happy that he decided to make a new start. "I will give half my money to the poor and I will repay those I have cheated," he said with a big smile.

Jesus was happy, too.

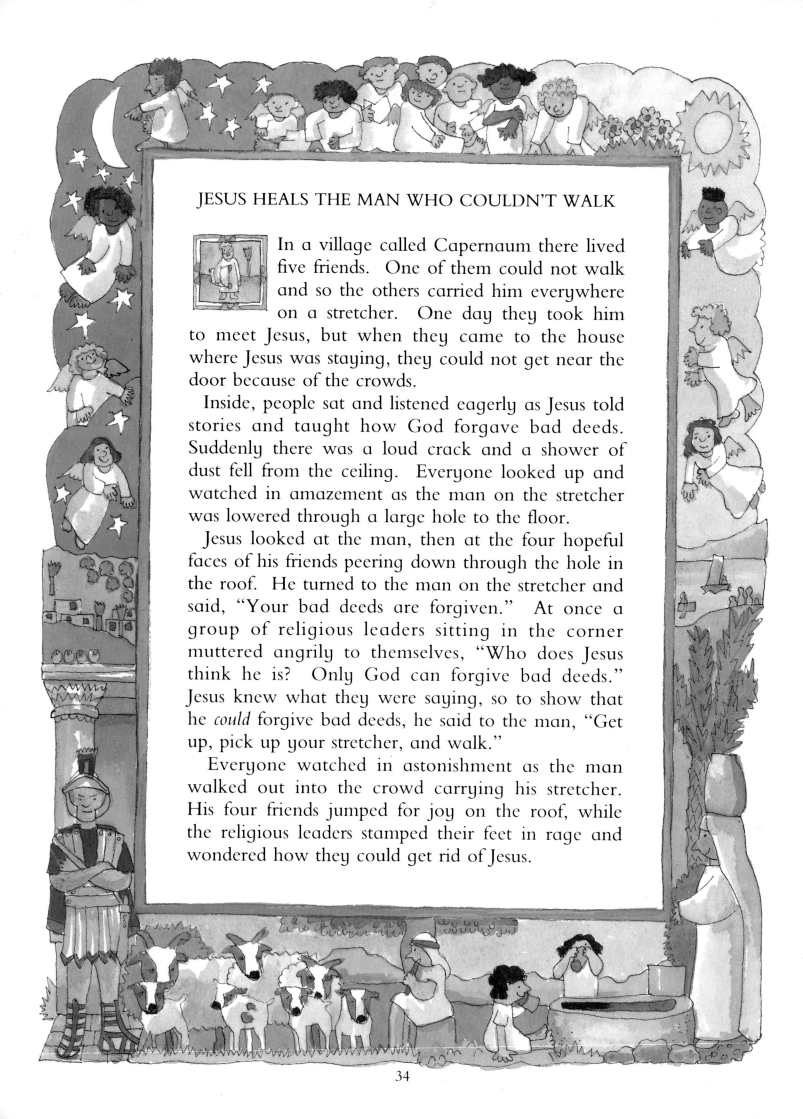

JESUS HEALS THE MAN WHO COULDN'T WALK

In a village called Capernaum there lived five friends. One of them could not walk and so the others carried him everywhere on a stretcher. One day they took him to meet Jesus, but when they came to the house where Jesus was staying, they could not get near the door because of the crowds.

Inside, people sat and listened eagerly as Jesus told stories and taught how God forgave bad deeds. Suddenly there was a loud crack and a shower of dust fell from the ceiling. Everyone looked up and watched in amazement as the man on the stretcher was lowered through a large hole to the floor.

Jesus looked at the man, then at the four hopeful faces of his friends peering down through the hole in the roof. He turned to the man on the stretcher and said, "Your bad deeds are forgiven." At once a group of religious leaders sitting in the corner muttered angrily to themselves, "Who does Jesus think he is? Only God can forgive bad deeds." Jesus knew what they were saying, so to show that he *could* forgive bad deeds, he said to the man, "Get up, pick up your stretcher, and walk."

Everyone watched in astonishment as the man walked out into the crowd carrying his stretcher. His four friends jumped for joy on the roof, while the religious leaders stamped their feet in rage and wondered how they could get rid of Jesus.

35

HOW JESUS ROSE FROM THE DEAD

It was a very busy time in Jerusalem. The Jews were getting ready for a festival called the Passover, when they remembered how God had saved their people in Egypt many years ago. Now the Jews hoped that God would save them from the Romans, too.

Jesus arrived in Jerusalem riding on a donkey, and the crowds thought that God had sent him to fight the Romans. They greeted him as if he were a king. They waved palm branches and shouted "Hosanna", which means "Save us now".

Now, there was a wise woman who knew that Jesus was no ordinary king. One evening she came to see him while he was having a meal with friends. They watched in silence as she poured expensive perfume over Jesus's head. (This was something that was usually done after a person had died.) Jesus's friends were cross. "What a waste of money," they grumbled. But Jesus explained that the woman was making his body ready for his death. When Judas, one of the disciples, heard this, he knew that Jesus was not going to fight the Romans after all. He was so disappointed that he went straight to the religious leaders. "I'll let you know where you can find Jesus," he said bitterly.

Jesus was very sad. He knew that Judas had turned against him.

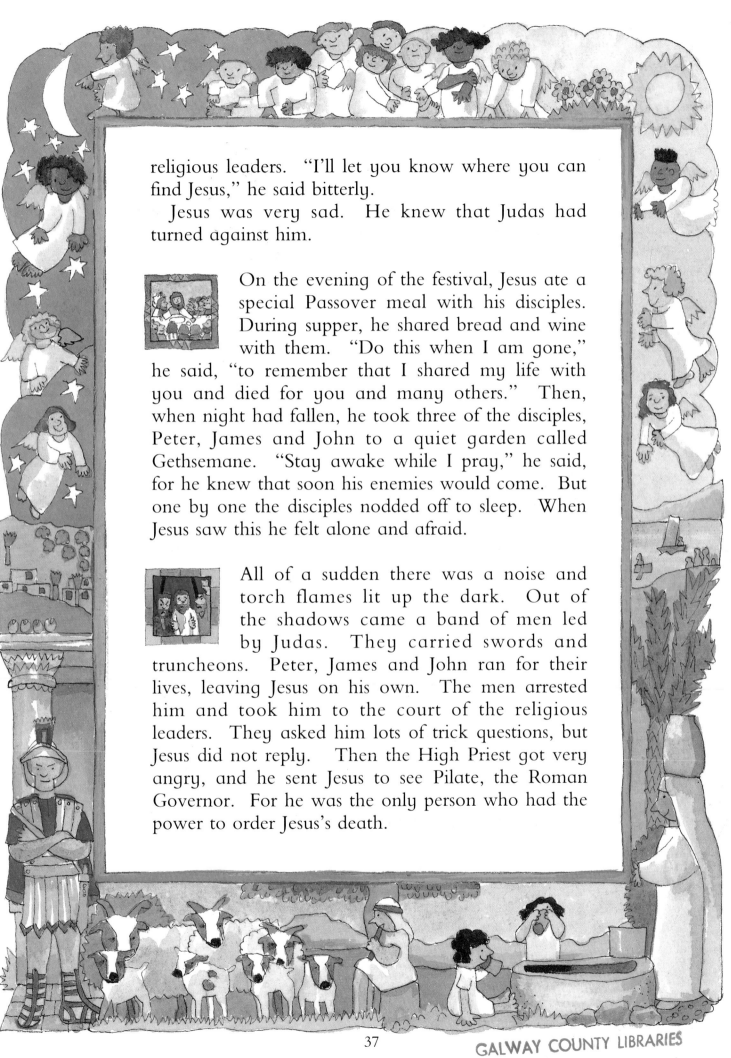

On the evening of the festival, Jesus ate a special Passover meal with his disciples. During supper, he shared bread and wine with them. "Do this when I am gone," he said, "to remember that I shared my life with you and died for you and many others." Then, when night had fallen, he took three of the disciples, Peter, James and John to a quiet garden called Gethsemane. "Stay awake while I pray," he said, for he knew that soon his enemies would come. But one by one the disciples nodded off to sleep. When Jesus saw this he felt alone and afraid.

All of a sudden there was a noise and torch flames lit up the dark. Out of the shadows came a band of men led by Judas. They carried swords and truncheons. Peter, James and John ran for their lives, leaving Jesus on his own. The men arrested him and took him to the court of the religious leaders. They asked him lots of trick questions, but Jesus did not reply. Then the High Priest got very angry, and he sent Jesus to see Pilate, the Roman Governor. For he was the only person who had the power to order Jesus's death.

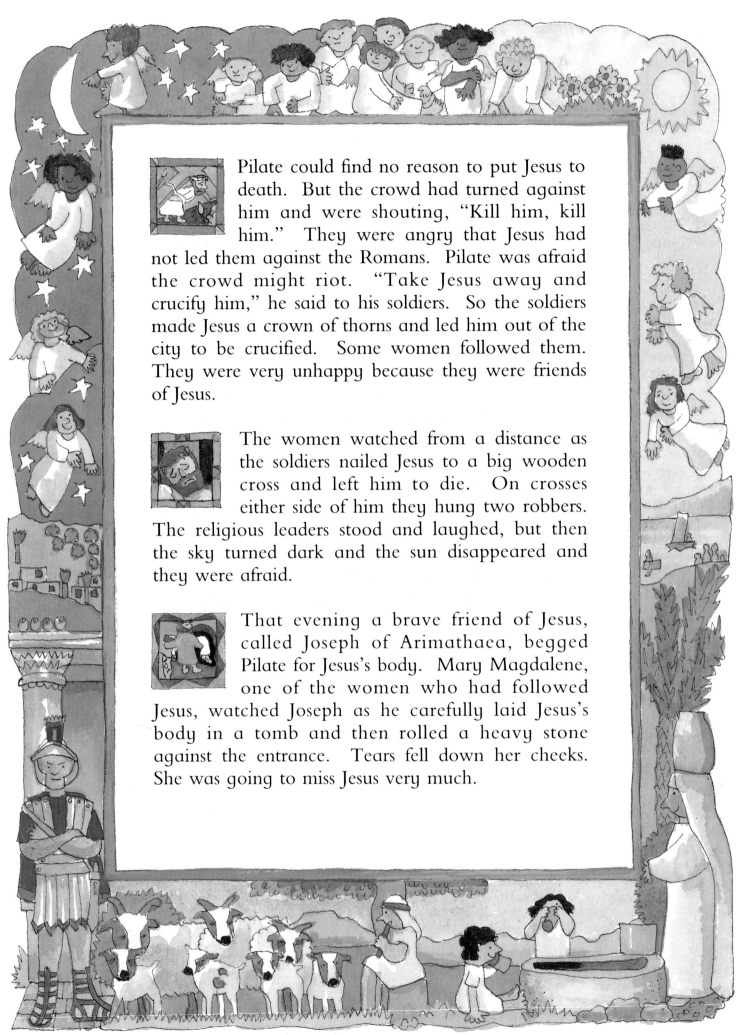

Pilate could find no reason to put Jesus to death. But the crowd had turned against him and were shouting, "Kill him, kill him." They were angry that Jesus had not led them against the Romans. Pilate was afraid the crowd might riot. "Take Jesus away and crucify him," he said to his soldiers. So the soldiers made Jesus a crown of thorns and led him out of the city to be crucified. Some women followed them. They were very unhappy because they were friends of Jesus.

The women watched from a distance as the soldiers nailed Jesus to a big wooden cross and left him to die. On crosses either side of him they hung two robbers. The religious leaders stood and laughed, but then the sky turned dark and the sun disappeared and they were afraid.

That evening a brave friend of Jesus, called Joseph of Arimathaea, begged Pilate for Jesus's body. Mary Magdalene, one of the women who had followed Jesus, watched Joseph as he carefully laid Jesus's body in a tomb and then rolled a heavy stone against the entrance. Tears fell down her cheeks. She was going to miss Jesus very much.

The next day was the sabbath, the day when Jews rested. Everything was quiet. Nothing moved. Very early on the following morning, before it was light, Mary went to the tomb. She was dismayed to find the stone had been rolled away from the entrance. "Someone has stolen his body," she cried to herself. Weeping, she bent down and peered into the tomb. Through her tears she saw two angels dressed in white. "Jesus's body has been taken away," she sobbed. Then she turned around and rubbed her eyes, because she saw someone standing in the darkness. She thought it must be the gardener, so she asked him urgently, "Is it you who has taken Jesus's body away?" The man said, "Mary," and at once Mary knew that it wasn't the gardener at all. It was Jesus! She was overjoyed, and hugged him tight. He was alive.

"Go and tell the disciples what you have seen," he said. So Mary went to tell them the good news.

Jesus had risen from the dead!